Providing Adolescent Foster Care

THINGS YOU SHOULD KNOW

Alphonso Kelly

ISBN: 978-1-963017-84-7

Printed in the United States of America

Contents

Preface

There are many less-fortunate children in our society who need good role models in their lives. It is said that "it takes a village to raise a child." Choosing to care for children who need love, comfort, and understanding in their lives can provide a wonderful feeling for the caregiver even if the children are not your biological children. Choosing to provide foster care can make a huge difference in a child's life! But be aware, there are serious negative aspects to foster care which can change your life forever! Your life could suffer emotional, financial and legal damage from which you may never fully recover.

This handbook is designed to be an informational guide for those who have contemplated providing adolescent foster care but did not know where to begin. In the following pages, I will provide insight to the world of adolescent foster care and examine the rewards as well as the perils of providing foster care. I will discuss fundamental skills necessary for good, effective parenting. Background environments and dysfunctional family structures of many children in foster care will also be discussed. Hopefully this book will provide insight on what to expect if you choose to travel this path.

Chapter 1

Getting Started

Many may wonder how and why people provide adolescent foster care. Well this is how it started for my wife Debbie and I. I met my wife in 1993 at a celebration party for the brother of a friend. We immediately connected and started dating a short time later. She was single and the mother of a sixteen year old boy and two teenage girls, ages eleven and thirteen. I was single and the father of a three year old son. We married a year later and everything was fine. We were one big, happy family.

As the teenagers grew older and began leaving home to go to college, our youngest son was left with no children at home to play with. Around this time some friends of ours were providing adolescent foster care and asked if we would be interested in providing foster care also. My wife and I discussed it and came to the conclusion that it would be a good idea because we could "kill two birds with one stone.. We would be providing an under privileged child with a good home and our son would have a foster brother tokeep him company. We just needed to know the process to get started. After lengthy research, we found that becoming licensed foster parents is not a short or easy process; there are many steps which must be taken.

You have the option to contract with your local Social Service Department or with a Child Placement Agency. Following the recommendation of our friends, we chose to contract with a Child Placement Agency because our friends were more familiar with this process and could perhaps provide us with some guidance.

To initiate to process, you are required to complete a child care license application through your state (as is the case in many states) as well as pay an application fee. Everyone in your household over the age of eighteen is required to complete an FBI background check and a state bureau of investigation fingerprint card. The background check is performed to determine if you have a history of domestic violence or child abuse. If you do have a have a history of domestic violence or child abuse, you are usually ineligible to obtain a child care license. Everyone in your household must have a current physical on file and you are required to complete a certain number of adolescent child care training hours per year as directed by your state and licensing agency. You have to be certified in first aid and CPR. Some agencies will provide these classes for your convenience. You have to obtain a medical administration certificate known as a QMAP (qualified medical administration provider) certificate because many of the foster children you encounter will be on some type of medication and you have to be qualified to administer their meds to them.

You need copies of your car and home owners insurance to show that your home and automobile(s) are insured in case of any accidents which may occur while foster children are in your care. Your home has to be inspected by your local fire department to ensure that your home meets local fire codes and does not have any fire safety violations. Fire extinguishers, that have been tested by a fire safety company within the last year, need to be hanging on the wall. Exit signs need to be posted on or over exit doors and exit routes need to be posted on each floor. Smoke and carbon monoxide detectors are also required to be on each floor, by bedrooms and in good working condition.

Your local health department will also inspect your home to make sure it is sanitary and provide you instruction regarding sanitary cooking and cleaning methods. They will also test your water and refrigerator temperature to make sure it is in the correct range. Your home will have to be inspected by your agency to ensure that your house is up-to-code for foster care. For example, your knives and sharp kitchen utensils need to be in a locked drawer or cabinet. Any chemicals such as alcohol and bleach also need to be locked away.

Some counties require a letter from any schools the kids will attend stating that it is ok for your foster children to attend their school. In some instances, you will need a letter from your local dentist and/or clinic stating that they will provide care for your foster children.

After your agency inspection is complete, the state will then conduct their inspection of your home or residence. They measure the bedrooms to make sure each child has a pre-determined amount of living space. They check to make sure all your required documents that need to be posted are posted. They check to make sure you had your fire and health department inspections completed. You also need monthly meal menus certified by a licensed dietitian and a list of emergency numbers and evacuation routes have to be posted on the wall or somewhere visible.

Once all inspections are passed and requirements are completed, you can expect to wait for four to eight weeks for your license to arrive. When it arrives, you post it on the wall also. Congratulations, you are now a certified foster home! Now the fun begins! Finding your first foster child!

Chapter 2

Child Selection

Figuring out how you go about getting matched with your first foster can be a confusing process when you are first getting started in foster care. There are so many questions you may have and not know where to get the answers. In this chapter, I will try to answer some of those questions and give you an idea of how to begin selecting your first foster child.

When my wife and I had completed all of our home inspections and were ready for our first foster child, we had no idea where to begin. We contracted with a child placement agency and they helped us through the process of getting a child into our home. However, there was still the question of what type of child was right for our home. This is one of the most important questions to answer. When we first started, our child placement agency would send us a list of children needing placement from various cities and counties in our state and we would look through the list and choose a kid without giving it much thought.. Big mistake! The child selection process is one of the most important decisions you make in foster care! It is imperative to know what type of child you want and determine what type of child would be a good "fit" in your household. If you don't do this, you could run into big problems early on.

You need to determine what age children you are interested in fostering. This is important for the social interaction of the children in your home. Children around the same age will generally have the same age appropriate development. When we received our first foster child in our home, my biological son was five and our foster son was ten. They got along and played together well, but there was a five year gap between them. Some things appropriate for a ten year old are not appropriate for a five year old. The next child we received was a seven year old boy. This allowed my biological son to have someone closer to his age to play with. It is always a good idea to have children interact with other kids close to their same age. When younger kids hang around with older kids, the younger kids start to think that they are older than their age and they can begin to learn bad habits from the older kids. On the flip side, older kids who frequently hang around with kids much younger than themselves tend to act younger than their age.

You also need to determine the sex and gender of the children you take. We found that it is not a good idea to mix foster boys and girls in the same home for obvious reasons; boys and girls who know they are not related tend to explore sexually when they think no one is watching. This occurs even more as the kids approach the age of puberty and beyond.

Another consideration is the race and nationality of the children you take into your home. Generally this does not matter to the child, but in some cases it does. We have had different races of children in our home at the same time and they got along reasonably well, but at times, racial issues and arguments would arise and have to be worked out once it came to our attention. When children come from different racial backgrounds and are used to different customs, they have to learn to adapt and accept others different from themselves. For example, one of my foster sons shared with me that he felt more comfortable in our home because he could relate to us racially.

Most importantly, you need to consider the reason placement is needed for the child. This is often the biggest factor you need to address when determining if a child will be a good fit for your home. When you receive the placement referral from the county, study it closely to determine why the child needs placement. If the referral does not contain enough information, call the caseworker of the child and ask as many questions as you can. This will save everyone a lot of time and headache. There are dozens of reasons foster children need placement and it is up to you to determine whether or not you can handle a particular child and his or her behaviors.

Many children need placement because of parental neglect such as drugs, domestic abuse, child abuse and abandonment. Some parents are also abused by out-of-control children due to a lack of parenting skills. Many parents of these children were very young when they had their first child and have no positive experience raising children, so you have children raising children. These young parents generally have no idea of how to correctly raise a child and often look to their mothers for guidance. If proper guidance is not available, the child may suffer and possibly be removed from the home by social services. Many of these homes are single parent homes where the father leaves and the mother is left alone to raise the child by herself.

Other cases involve children who are physically and verbally abused by one or both parents. Many of these parents are addicted to drugs and openly engage in all types of deviant behavior in front of their children. Many of these children enter the foster care system full of remorse and resentment. They may be angry at social services for removing them from their homes and angry at their parents for causing it to happen. These children can also be very sad because they are usually separated from their siblings once they enter the social service system. Social Services makes an effort to keep sibling groups together and return them to their homes if their parents conform to treatment plans, but this is not always successful.

While children wait for their parent(s) to conform to treatment plans, the children may be housed in residential treatment centers or youth detention centers. They generally remain in these centers until a lower level of care (such as a group home, group center or foster home) can be found. Many children learn bad habits and behaviors while in these centers and bring these characteristics with them to their new foster home. That is why it is very important to know the background of any child you consider taking into your home. This information will help you evaluate whether or not you can handle this child living in your home and give you insight to the child's behaviors so you can have an idea of what to expect once the child enters your home.

Your child placement agency or county agency will generally contact you and give you a referral for a child needing foster care placement. It is a good idea to call the child's caseworker and ask as many questions as you can think of about the child before deciding to meet with the child. Caseworkers may withhold negative information about a child because they want you to take the child into your home so make sure you ask plenty of questions.

Once you do decide to meet with a potential candidate for your home, it is a good idea to meet at a location other than your home. The social service office or the child's housing facility usually will suffice. This is done to afford you and the child the opportunity to meet without the distraction of where you live. You don't want the child to want to come live with you just because you have a nice house. This happened to us once when we first started doing foster care. We met the child at our house and the child was so excited that he didn't want to leave after the interview. Later his caseworker told us that the child threw a tantrum and ran off down the street as she was returning him to his residential treatment facility. We had agreed to take him in at the meeting and he was excited about coming to our home, but he did not want to wait for the paperwork to be processed. We learned that meeting at a neutral location helps with the transition time.

Children can remain in foster care until they are allowed to return home, get adopted or reach the age of emancipation. This can take weeks, months or years so prepared yourself accordingly.

Chapter 3

Happy Anniversary

After all the paperwork is signed, bags are packed and the child moves into his/her new home, then the fun begins! You introduce your new foster son/daughter to the rest of the family and help them move into their new room. After they are unpacked and settled in, it is a great idea to have a meeting with your new foster son/daughter to go over the house rules and expectations. This should occur as soon as possible as this is a key element in establishing structure in your household.

Your foster son or daughter now knows the rules and expectations of the house and things usually go smoothly for two to four weeks. This is known as the "Anniversary" period. The child usually displays his or her best behavior during this time. He or she is still becoming acquainted with their new surroundings and they are still "feeling you out" and trying to be pleasant. After this transition period, the child becomes more relaxed and their normal behaviors begin to emerge. This is the time to be very consistent with the rules and structure of your home and above all, teach and emphasize respect.

Many foster children come from dysfunctional homes with little or no appropriate family structure. They have no idea of how to respect their elders, peers or themselves. It is now your job as their foster parent to teach them. This may sound easy to do but it's not; It takes lots of practice and discipline. Some parents tend to be friends with their kids first and parents second. This is a big mistake! Children need parents first for guidance and structure and stability. Their friends are the ones who provide comradery and socialization. Children may not always be able to count on their friends, but they should always be able to count on their parents.

Parents may not always be popular with their children; however they should always have their respect. If you as a parent do not instill respect in your child, he or she will find it hard to respect anyone else; whether it be their teachers at school, their boss at work or any other authority figure because they have not learned to respect authority at home. If kids see you as a friend first and a parent second, they will show you a friendship level of respect instead of a parental level of respect and it will end up hurting them in the long run.

When the child does something wrong, it will make your job as a parent easier if to hold them accountable for their actions every time and are consistent with consequences. You must be consistent otherwise the lessons you are teaching will not be ingrained in them. It may seem like your kids don't like you at times - because no kid likes to be punished - but in the long run they will appreciate you for remaining consistent. We have seen it time and time again with the children we have raised when others adults compliment us on how well-behaved and respectful our children are. Often, when my wife and I go to parent/ teacher conferences for our kids, the teachers tell us how respectful our children are. Even if the teacher has a complaint they may say, "John needs to turn in all of his homework but over all, he's pleasant to have in class and very respectful." Respect for others and accountability are invaluable lessons children need to learn while growing up at home. If they don't learn it at home, society will teach it to them in much harsher ways than their parents; Jails and prisons are full of young men and women who never learned respect for rules and laws. This often leads back to how they were raised. If children do not learn to be respectful and accountable as children, they will not know how to be respectful and accountable as adults and it will cost them (and perhaps you) in the long run. Respect and accountability are two leading factors which determine good or bad behavior in children. Teach these traits early on and life will be a lot easier for you and your children.

As a foster parent, you need to learn the tricks of the trade when dealing with children. You can be assured that children know how to manipulate you and will push the boundaries. Children will always try to get what they want and try different ploys to achieve their goal. If you don't know and recognize them already, learn and correct them immediately as they occur. The following are a few examples of how a child might try to get what they want.

If you are a two parent household, the child will ask one parent for permission to do or have something. If that parent says no, the child goes to the other parent and asks the same thing. This is known as "playing two sides against the middle." The child needs to be made aware that you and your spouse or significant other are unified when it comes to decision making and that trying to get a yes from another parent when they have already been told no will not be tolerated.

Foster children will also try to play "two sides against the middle" with you and their caseworkers. The child may not like the rules of your house and try to "tell on you" to their caseworkers thinking that their caseworkers override your house rules. When this occurs, you, the child and his or her caseworker need to meet and inform the child that the adults are on the same page and are in agreement. If you find that you and a child's caseworker are not in agreement where the child is concerned, it is a good idea to have the child moved elsewhere. If the adults are not working together in the best interest of the child and you are dealing with a caseworker who thinks that the child knows what is in his or her own best interest then it is a good idea to have the caseworker relocate the child elsewhere. It is your house and your rules so if those you allow to come live in your house can't follow the rules then they should not be there. It does not work that way in society and your home should be no different. If a child breaks the rules at school, he or she will be suspended or expelled. If the child breaks the law, he or she will go to juvenile detention or jail. The child needs to be prepared for the realities of life and not fooled into believing in a false sense of reality which the social service system often provides.

Some children will ask repeatedly for something hoping that their persistence will cause you to change your mind. When you make a decision, stand by it and don't be swayed. Let the child know that your answer is final and that trying to make you change your mind will not be tolerated. If you allow the child to beg you into changing your decision, he or she will realize that you are not confident in your decisions and your child will try to change your mind all the time when they don't get what they want. Teach your child that no means no and to respectfully accept your decision without anger or pouting. Explain to them that people don't always get what they want. If they learn this early in life, they will be better equipped to handle situations that don't go their way in the future.

Chapter 4

Medication & Children

There are literally thousands of children in need of foster care and many are diagnosed with numerous disorders such as ADHD, ADD, Bipolar disorder, depression or other mental illness and behavior isssues. Often times the institutional method for addressing these disorders is to prescribe medication. As a society, we tell our kids to say "No" to drugs, yet we have a drug for almost every ailment and negative emotion. Drugs or "medications" are given to children at very young ages for even minor behavioral problems. Then society expects kids to differentiate between "good" or medically necessary drugs and "bad" or recreational drugs. Many children will not understand the difference and will see all drugs as a remedy for whatever ails them in life and they may use them as an easy escape from reality.

In my opinion, most drugs given to children are for behavior modification and are used because it is easier to prescribe a pill than use older, traditional methods of discipline. Structure, discipline, accountability and daily exercise seem to be things of the past, however they seemed to worked much better than modern day solutions. When I was growing up, if you had an abundance of energy your parent(s) enrolled you in some type of sport or made you go outside to play and burn off energy. This solution allowed you to get exercise and burn off energy without having to ingest a chemical substance with unknown long or short term side effects! If you wet the bed, your mom or dad would train you to have better bladder control by limiting liquid intake before bed or even wake you up to use the toilet during the night. If you seemed sad or depressed, your parents would spend time talking to you to make you feel better.

The majority of foster children who entered our home were on some type of medication and in special education classes in school. Over time, with the use of traditional methods of discipline and by building relationship with them, many of our foster children no longer needed medication (verified by their physicians) and were moved out of special education classes into mainstream classes. Some even made the honor roll and went to college.

Be prepared, the majority of children who enter your home will already be on one or more medications and have a variety of behavioral problems. You will need to determine the best way to mitigate these problems and stabilize the child. We accomplished this by making our children accountable for their actions and limiting excuses. We also taught them to have respect for themselves and others and held them to higher standards and expectations than they typically asked of them. For example, we worked hard to instill personal accountability in our foster children. We found that many of our foster children would blame everything and everyone else for their behavior They were masters at not incriminating themselves. Whenever we questioned them about any trouble they got into at school, or at home for that matter, the reason was always someone else's fault. Our kids would never tell the whole story and we identified a pattern of lack of accountability. They would say things like: "That teacher doesn't like me" or "I was sitting in my seat and the teacher started yelling at me for no reason." This is why it is very important to get both sides of the story and recount the events of the incident with the child step-by-step. The child will try to avoid taking responsibility for their actions, so it is critical that the child acknowledges why they got in trouble and how their choices played a part. You have to let them know that you are smart enough to know that they did not get yelled at or punished by the teacher for merely sitting in their seats minding their own business. Once the child knows that you have talked to the teacher and know more facts than he or she is giving you, it is easier to get to the bottom of what really happened. Then the story changes to, "I was asking my friend for a piece of paper when I was supposed to be quietly taking a test" or "I just got out of my seat for a minute to throw something away and I got in trouble". This is the accountability the child needs to acknowledge to begin positive growth. Once you get the child to acknowledge his or her contribution to the events of the problem, you can then teach them how making better choices can help them avoid future problems.

There must also be consequences for each indiscretion. The punishments should start out light and increase in duration and severity if the negative behavior persists. For instance, the first offense may result in missing a few hours of television and video game playing. Subsequent offenses may result in no television or video games for the whole weekend (and so on). This takes practice and consistency, but it works like a charm! You will soon notice that your children get into less trouble at school and their behavior begins to improve once they learn to be accountable for their actions. When your children become adults, society is going to hold them to these same standards with far greater sanctions for breaking the law. Don't think you are doing your kids any favors by letting them get away with breaking rules. Not your rules, the schools rules or any rules because what you fail to teach them now, society will teach them later; And with far greater consequences. I always tell my sons that it doesn't matter if others are misbehaving, always strive to follow the rules and do the right thing and you will reap the benefits in the long run.

Chapter 5

Raising Children Properly

I felt compelled to include this chapter because I strongly believe that it is the most important component of providing foster care or any other type of child care. The knowledge of how to properly raise children and the ability to consistently use that knowledge is a key factor in determining whether or not you will be a successful parent, foster or otherwise. It is your job as a parent to do what is in the best interest of the child. Raising your child to be a productive member of society is not only in the child's best interest but in society's best interest as a whole.

There are an increasing number of people who are raising or attempting to raise children who have no idea of how to raise a child properly. There are many reasons for this. Some people never learned proper child raising techniques from their parents so when they find become parents, they have no idea how to do it correctly and the child ends up raising themselves. Some people who are raising children are children themselves because of their age. They have no idea of proper child rearing techniques because they are in adolescent stages of development themselves. Others have a desire to raise children by providing foster care or adoption and have no child raising experience other than what they have been told or have read in books. Whatever the circumstance, raising children correctly is of utmost importance.

We have all seen people in public whose children are running amuck, jumping and climbing over everything and thought to ourselves, "Wow, those kids are out of control! Then we look and see their parent(s) idly sitting by acting as if that type of behavior is acceptable. Apparently, kids are supposed to be jumping over office furniture, standing on tables and rolling around on filthy public floors! The kids scream at the top of their lungs when they want something and put their filthy public floor hands in their mouths! Their parents seem to think that this is normal child behavior and make no effort to correct their children. If their children are frequently ill, these parents don't correlate the ingestion of germs, bacteria and viruses with sickness. Then when their children are at school and don't know how to sit still, pay attention and listen to the teacher, these parents blame the teachers. It is not the teachers' job alone to teach children proper and appropriate behavior. Some parents may think that their children will simply grow out of bad and disruptive behavior over time. Or they might believe their kids are "just being kids." Unfortunately, children usually don't "grow out" of bad behavior. Without any altering factors, as the child grows, so does the behavior. Minor, adolescent misbehavior often becomes, harmful adult behavior. So it is important to correct the behavior while young children are still teachable and you have the opportunity.

My wife and I have met many potential adoptive parents who were interested in adopting and raising a child for the first time. A few of these parents in particular were very committed to adopting a child. The problem was they had no prior experience. We stressed the importance experience plays in raising children and suggested that they either start off by providing foster care or getting a child who is fairly young in age and has not been in the social service system very long. We explained to these potential adoptive parents that getting a young child (below the age of 7) would allow the parents to have a better chance at molding the child and instilling in them their rules and expectations. The younger the child is, the easier it is to teach them your expectations because they have not begun to develop the independent thought patterns that older children have begun to develop.

Getting matched with a child who has not been indoctrinated into the social service system is a huge benefit because you don't have to deal with the negative habits and manipulative behaviors the child learns from other children when they are housed together in residential treatment centers or other locations they have been placed in by the department of social services.

At the time, the children that these potential parents where looking to adopt were teenagers, or would be teenagers soon and were living in a (our) group home. These particular children had been in the social service system for several years and had multiple failed home placements. The fact that these children were in group homes and had several previous failed placements was an indication that they required a higher level of care and experience to raise. It seemed that no matter how long we talked to these potential adoptive parents or how much advice we gave them, they were dead-set on doing it their way. They would tell us things like, "We have been reading books and feel confident that we are ready" or "We saw the child playing at the adoption exchange and liked the way he looked. We can't wait to get him in our home!"

Unfortunately, the potential parents found that out the hard way that brining teenage children who have been in the child welfare system for an extended amount of time is not easy, to say the least.

The children's caseworkers would come to our house and ask my wife and I what we thought about the adoptive parent(s) and the child being adopted. We would tell the caseworkers that even though we were in favor of the child having the opportunity to be adopted; it is a bad idea to de-stabilize a high level kid by moving him in with parents who have no child rearing experience. One caseworker told us that she had the highest level of confidence in the adoptive parent's ability to successfully raise a child from a group home; even with no experience. I asked the caseworker why she had more confidence in a potential adoptive parent with no child raising experience than she had in the advice of two foster/biological parents with more than 30 years of child raising experience. The caseworker had no answer to this question and proceeded with the adoption. A single, white female with no child raising experience attempting to raise two African-American, teenage boys on her own sounds like a recipe for disaster to me! I guess time will tell.

As for the other potential adoptive parents; the move was a disaster and they returned the child to social services more damaged than when they received him. The child proved to be much more than they could handle and the child was sent to a residential treatment center (which is a higher level of care than a group home) and back on medication and therapy! He was off medication, off therapy, and had progressed from special education classes to the honor roll at the time his caseworker chose to move him in with potential adoptive parents with no experience. These are just some of the frustrations you may face when providing foster care because situations like this occur all the time. Once you begin to stabilize your foster child, the county tries to lower the child's level of care before the child is stable enough to maintain that level on their own. If the child's new caregivers are not experienced enough to provide an adequate level of structure and discipline, the child often reverts back to their old habits and behaviors very quickly. This often causes a failed placement as the child may be removed from the home and placed back into a higher level of care which can have a detrimental impact on the child's self esteem. Therefore, it is very important to have adequate knowledge and experience in regards to raising children if you want to raise them successfully.

Chapter 6

No Credit

When a new foster child enters your home they typically come with a variety of bad habits and behaviors that need to be corrected. As a result of their behavior issue, the child is usually in special education classes at. The child may also have numerous services in place, such as therapy and medication, to help the child function on a daily basis. Even with these services in place the child usually still struggles to stay on task and may fail to advance in school or at home. The best way to get these children back on track is to immediately begin teaching them character building principles such as respect, honor, discipline and self control, to name a few. Many foster children have no idea what these characteristics mean and it will be up to you to teach them.

Many foster children have spent several years observing and learning bad, dysfunctional behaviors and it will be up to you, as their foster parent, to help them relearn positive behaviors. It took time for these children to learn these negative behaviors and it will take time to erase them and teach them new, positive ones. Teaching a child how to respect their teachers, their peers and themselves is a long, slow, arduous task to say the least. This will require multiple hours of talking with your child about the right and wrong ways to do something. It requires teaching by example because what a child sees has as much, if not more, impact on them as what he or she hears. "Do as I say, not as I do" does not work because the child will believe if the behavior is good enough for you, it's good enough for them. It is of great importance to be consistent with the lessons you teach your children and the example you set. If you waver in your teachings your child will be inconsistent in learning the lessons you are trying to teach. The child will attempt to resist learning your lessons so you must be consistent or you will most likely fail. After months of consistently teaching your foster child these new principles, they will begin to emulate them at school. You will begin to notice a positive change in their behavior and their teachers and caseworkers will also notice.

This is when the "no credit" part begins. Many foster children who are in special education classes at school have an I.E.P (Individual Education Plan). The child's teachers, caseworkers and foster parent(s) generally meet at different times throughout the school year to discuss the child's progress and determine if the child still needs special education services. If your teachings have been consistent and your foster child's academic development was not related to bad behavior, they may no longer need special education classes. This usually makes the child and the I.E.P team very happy because it shows that the child has made significant positive progress at school. The child may also be happy for several other reasons as well. She may have felt stigmatized because she needed special education classes when most of her friends did not. The child may also be happy to be in general education classes and not have the feeling of being less intelligent than other students. As a foster parent, you may feel overlooked by the I.E.P staff because some of them will attribute the child's success and progress to the child's efforts alone. This is where it gets dangerous for the child. Your foster child's caseworker and G.A.L may believe that because the child is progressing behaviorally and academically she should be moved to a lower level of care which means removing the child from your home. This could be disastrous for the child. The caseworkers and G.A.Ls often overlook the fact that your foster child is still a work in progress. Another home or location may not be able to pick up where you left off with your foster child and the child may rapidly regress to old, negative behaviors and habits without the stability they have found in your home and what you have taught them.

Chapter 7

SCHEDULE & ACTIVITIES

It is a good idea to have a household schedule and routine in place that includes recreational activities for you foster children when they arrive at your home. Keeping your kids enrolled in healthy activities is a key component to running a successful home. Schedules and activities such as club and team sports provide exercise for your child and help teach them structure and discipline. Children learn valuable lessons such as cooperation, leadership and team spirit when involved in extra-curricular activities. They also become proud of their achievements and physical attributes that develop from exercise.

We enrolled our kids in track and field, football and the local gym. Our kids went from being out of shape to being the most fit kids in their classes and on their teams. The more our kids achieved, the more they wanted to achieve. One of our sons broke eight track and field records in three states in one year at the age of 12. Another son scored 20 touchdowns in one football season. Over the years our foster children placed in the top ranks of the Amateur Athletic Union (AAU) and United States Track & Field (USATF) tournaments around the country.. Some even went to college on athletic scholarships and some received academic scholarships as well. . Activities are highly recommended and can do wonders for a child's moral and self worth. A few of our foster kids were so surprised and happy when they made the honor role at school that they began competing to see who could get the best grades. All these achievements began with a strict schedule and structured activities. There are several after-school activities children can participate in such as basketball, soccer, wrestling, tennis, track and field, football, and others. Just find out which sport or activity your children are most interested in and get them involved.

Of course you will find that children are generally excited to be involved in a sport or club in the beginning. However when the activity begins to get hard and not all about fun, some kids will want to quit and do something else. It is very important to keep them focused and on track. Explain to your kids that everything worthwhile takes hard work and determination. They will not succeed in life by quitting when things get difficult.

A former foster child of ours used to hate track and would often complain about it while he lived with us. He eventually left our home and was returned to his biological mother's residence. He called us a few years later and thanked us for keeping him involved in track and field. He ended up running track at his high school and did very well. He shared with us that he liked the calming effect that running provided for him; when he and his mother had tense moments he would go for a run to calm his nerves. Even though he said that he hated running track when he lived with us, track turned out to be his main source of comfort when he got older. Many of our children were able to attain their goals later in life by using the lessons that extra-curricular activities provide. Hopefully, yours will also.

Chapter 8

The Dark Side

I titled this chapter "The Dark Side" because it covers some of the negative aspects of foster care. While foster care can be rewarding for foster children and foster parents, it can also become a very negative and painful experience for both the child and the foster parent.

 For the child who finds him or herself in foster care, life can be very traumatic and depressing. One day, the child is living at home with his biological family and the next day the child finds him or herself in the custody of the department of social services surrounded by strangers. Although the circumstances for the child being removed from his/her biological family may be legitimate and in the child's best interest, the child still suffers a sense of loss and betrayal. Even though a child's home life may have been rough and full of neglect by their biological parents, he/she still sees their home as a place of permanency. When this permanency is removed, the child often blames their biological parents for not providing adequate care for them and allowing them to be removed from their home.

Children can remain in the custody of the department of Social Services for weeks, months, or years depending on the severity of the neglect case against their parents. Many children are returned to their biological parent(s) if their parents successfully complete the requirements social service has for them. Many of these same children return to the custody of the department of social services when their biological parents revert back to their old habits and the pattern of neglect resumes.

After being in the social services system, many children get used to moving from various residential treatment centers and foster homes. Some of these children have had over 20 placements. The department of social services continues to look for permanency for these children either by returning them home to their biological parents or looking for a family relative to care for them. If returning the child to a family member is unsuccessful, the department of social services will generally attempt to find adoptive parents for the child. If this is unsuccessful the child may be placed in long term foster care or in a residential treatment center (RTC). The child could remain in a RTC or in foster care until they emancipate.

For a child, being shuffled from place to place and not having a stable home can be traumatic and depressing. For this reason, many children are placed in therapy and prescribed various medications. As a foster parent it is very important to know the case history of any child you contemplate accepting into your home so you have knowledge of their past experiences. This information will help you better understand various behavioral patterns and issues the child may have before entering your home.

Once children enter your home and the honeymoon phase has passed, they often become complacent and tend to forget about previous placements. This is where problems can begin for you as a foster parent. You may notice that as long as your foster child displays good behavior and has privileges, he/she can seem happy as can be with no signs of sadness or depression. But as soon as your child does get into trouble and sanctions are imposed, your home becomes the pit of despair and the child wants to call his caseworker and request to be moved to another placement. After getting into trouble and receiving a punishment, children always seem to think that the "grass is greener" elsewhere. Unfortunately, some caseworkers will act on the child's request and move them to another placement. In similar situations , my wife and I always explain to the caseworkers that the adults have to work together for the good of the child. If the child is allowed to manipulate the system every time he/she gets in trouble, then our house is not the right placement for them. We also explain to the child and their caseworker that if the child runs away or is moved by the caseworker, they will not be allowed to return to our home and his placement will be filled by another child. This is to discourage the "revolving door" syndrome where a child leaves your home and decides to return after discovering that the "grass is not greener" elsewhere. This tends to happen frequently so be prepared.

Another play foster children use after being punished for breaking rules is to make a false allegation. This is perhaps the most troublesome and irritating occurrence for a foster parent. Your foster child may try to retaliate against you for punishing her by making a false claim to her caseworker in an attempt to get you in trouble. This is a very serious occurrence because when an allegation is made by a child, your county and state licensing agencies will conduct an immediate investigation of your residence in an attempt to protect the child from possible harm. The person(s) who are vulnerable during an investigation are the foster parents because, whether the allegation is true or false, your family will be placed under a microscope. This can be very disruptive and damaging to a foster families' reputation because it casts a shadow of doubt on you and your family where none had existed before. Your foster child is aware of this. Often, the biological family of the foster child knows this also and will try to use false allegations against you in an attempt to get their child removed from your home and returned to them.

When an accusation is make, the counties' child neglect department will immediately conduct an investigation of your home. Then your state licensing agency will conducts a follow-up investigation as well. A state investigator once shared that allegations are commonplace for those providing foster care.

However, there is no "common" feel about it. During an investigation, it seems like you are presumed guilty because everyone in your household and anyone deemed relevant to the case is interviewed. During the interviews, the investigator tries to find any incriminating evidence against you. If they are unable to find any evidence, they generally say that the allegation was inconclusive instead of unfounded. An inconclusive ruling makes it seem like you could be guilty but they just couldn't find enough evidence. Even if the child has a history of false allegations, the investigators rarely says that the accusations were unfounded. An unfounded ruling makes you look possibly guilty and can cause serious damage to your reputation. As a result, other counties may see this on your record and be hesitant to place children with you in the future.

Chapter 9
STORIES

I'll share with you some accounts of children who made false allegations against their foster homes or thought that "the grass would be greener" elsewhere.

Tom

There was one little boy, who I will call "Tom", who came to a group home from a higher level of care residential treatment center. When Tom arrived at the group home he was taking multiple medications for various behavioral problems. Tom was in special education classes at school and was scheduled to see a therapist once a week. Because of his severe behavior problems he was not a candidate for adoption.

After living in the group home for nearly two years with experienced foster parents, Tom's behavior improved greatly. He no longer had to take his previously prescribed medications because it was demonstrated to his physician that Tom could successfully function on a day to day basis without them. He no longer had to see a therapist every week and his behavior at school improved so much that Tom was removed from the self-contained, special education classroom and placed in mainstream classes. Tom's grades went from D's and F's to A's and B's. Tom also made the honor role for the first time in his life and was even placed in some advanced classes. He also excelled on his track team! Tom was very proud of his accomplishments and so were his foster parents. In a stable environment and consistent parenting, Tom's behavior had dramatically improved.

Tom's behavior had improved so much that he was now eligible for adoption and placed on an adoption web site for exposure to potential adoptive parents. Tom's caseworker believed that he was ready to transition from his group home to an adoptive home, so the county (Dept. of Social Services) assigned an adoption caseworker to Tom's case. Tom was very excited when he heard that there was a possibility for him to be adopted! Even though he was doing very well in his present foster home, the anticipation of being adopted and moving somewhere new was inciting.

The adoption caseworker arranged several outings for Tom to attend. The purpose an outing is to give potential adoptive parents an opportunity to observe foster children (without the children's knowledge) and choose a child of their liking. At one such outing, a married couple took a liking to Tom and expressed an interest in adopting him. Tom's caseworker informed the foster parents about the potential adoptive parents' interest in adopting Tom and asked for their opinion on the matter. Tom's foster parents believed that Tom could only be successful in a new home if his new parents were experienced and knowledgeable enough to provide the same structure and discipline Tom was receiving in their home and his caseworker initially agreed. When the potential adoptive parents revealed that they had no prior child rearing experience, Tom's foster parents informed the caseworker that choosing this couple to adopt Tom would be a huge mistake. They reiterated the importance that experience and knowledge played in raising a child like Tom. His foster parents knew this better than anyone. After all, they were the ones who raised Tom the previous two years; they were the ones responsible for helping to improve Tom's behavior. They were also the ones who taught Tom the discipline and study habits that enabled him to move from special education classes to general education classes .

After hearing all the recommendations and warnings from Tom's foster parents, his caseworker decided to move him in with the inexperienced adoptive parents anyway. Tom's foster parents met several times with the adoptive parents to share parenting advice and discipline techniques that worked well with Tom. The foster parents also suggested that the adoptive parents try being foster parents first or even possibly adopt a younger child who required a lower level of care. They explained that they wanted Tom's adoption to be successful and believed that attempting to adopt a child who required a high level of care would be unsuccessful without adequate experience. The adoptive parents believed that they were up for the challenge and were very excited and anxious for Tom to move in with them.

When the day arrived for Tom to move in with his new adoptive family, his foster parents wished them well and instructed Tom to remember what he had learned from them and to continue to be good. Unfortunately, the scenario played out just as Tom's foster parents feared it would. Tom was fine in his new home for the first month (the anniversary period). Then Tom's old behaviors began to return and his new, inexperienced adoptive parents found out that parenting was much harder than they had anticipated; especially with child who required a high-level of Tom's behavior had steadily improved with his foster parents because they had the necessary experience to provide adequate structure and discipline for Tom. Once Tom moved into his new home with his adoptive parents, he found that he could easily manipulate them because of their lack of experience. Within a few months Tom had reverted back to disrespectful and defiant behaviors. After only four months, Tom's adoptive parents decided that they could not handle him. They cancelled the adoption and returned Tom to the department of social services. Tom was moved to various group homes and residential treatment centers. He was also prescribed medication and therapy again in an attempt to re-stabilize him to no avail. Just as Tom's foster parents had feared, he was moved from a stable environment to an unstable and because of inexperience Tom was the one who ultimately suffered.

Chris

There was another kid, who I will call Chris, who suffered a similar fate as Tom. Chris had been in foster care for half of his life and had resided in multiple foster homes, group homes and residential treatment centers. He had developed many bad habits from as a result of his various placements and required a high level of care. His profile report was dozens of pages thick and listed several negative behaviors and personality traits such as excessive lying, stealing, fighting, bed-wetting, truancy, defiance and fire setting, to name a few. In fact, Chris's profile report was so bad that his county had difficulty finding a new placement for him when they deemed him ready to "step down" to a lower level of care.

At the time, my wife and I had an opening in our group home and received Chris's referral from our child placement agency. We generally don't accept kids into our group home who have a history of sexual behavior or fire setting. This is by design to help protect us and others in our home from these two known dangers which are hard to break and can have deadly consequences. Chris' referral did not mention many of his negative habits or past behaviors so we agreed to meet with Chris and his caseworker for an intake interview. During the interview we discovered other issues that were purposely left out of Chris' profile referral in order to get someone to consider accepting him into their home. But after meeting with Chris and his caseworker, my wife and I decided to give him a chance and accepted him into our home. Chris and his caseworker were very happy with our decision and he moved in a few days later.

When Chris arrived, my wife and I went over the rules of the house with him and enrolled him in school. Not unlike other children in foster care, Chris was in special education classes, prescribed multiple medications and attended therapy. We knew we had our work cut out for us. We discovered that Chris could barely read and would cry if made to do so. His hygiene was awful and he liked to play with fire. At school, Chris was defiant with teachers and placed in a special education, "self contained" classroom with other children who had behavioral problems. Chris began "acting out" even before the customary 30 day anniversary period was over so my wife and I knew we had a lot of work to do to get Chris on the right track. Fortunately for us, Chris had a very good and supportive caseworker who had worked on his case for years. Chris' caseworker agreed to support us in our effort to get his life on track. This was very important because if the adults in a child's life don't work together, it will be very difficult to make progress with the child. Chris behavior was so bad when he arrived in our home that he was not being considered for adoption (as is the case with many children who enter our home).

Through years of diligent work, Chris gradually began learning to respect himself and others. His grades began to improve and he was eventually moved from special education to general education classes. He also no longer required medication or therapy. All this was accomplished by consistently teaching and displaying positive structure and discipline to Chris. Chris' improved behavior soon made him eligible for the adoption list and he was very happy and excited when he heard the news. Chris had always wanted to be adopted but his behavior had always kept him off the adoption list. Now he had a chance.

Unfortunately for Chris, becoming eligible for adoption meant that he would be assigned a new caseworker, an adoption caseworker, who did not know any of us and was not familiar with the hard work it took to get Chris to his current behavioral level.

The adoption caseworker did not seem to be working with Chris' best interest in mind. She felt that if Chris was successful at our house, he could be successful elsewhere. She also said that she believed Chris needed more freedom and a lower level of care. I suspect she was interested in relocating Chris to a foster home closer to their county so she would not have to make the hour long drive each month. She would meet with Chris at school without our knowledge and tell him that he would be moving soon. Chris was very excited to hear this. Like many other children, he fell victim to "the grass is greener elsewhere" syndrome My wife and I explained to Chris and his adoption caseworker that they should consider moving slowly because Chris would likely have to self-disciplined and learn to stay on track. We would not be there to remind him and his room at our group home would probably not be available if they changed their mind later. We also informed the caseworker that although Chris' behavior had improved greatly, he still would require experienced, caring adults to keep him on track.

The adoption caseworker moved Chris anyway and we did not hear from him. Then a few months later, Chris called us and said that his new placement had failed because of behavioral problems and he was now back living in a residential treatment center. Basically, Chris was back to square one. He was back on medication and in therapy again all because the social service system fails to let children who are becoming stable remain in the environment that provided them the stability. As soon as a child begins to stabilize, social services de-stabilizes them by moving them to a lower level of care. They say that it is not based on financial considerations, but I find it hard to justify their decisions otherwise. Chris is no longer on the adoption list and is facing long-term foster care until the age of emancipation.

Name

Race can play a role in foster care placement as well. I have an African-American friend (named Emma) who ran a girls group home where she generally housed African-American girls. She occasionally received referrals for Hispanic and Caucasians girls as well. My friend never gave much thought to a child's nationality because she figured that kids are kids who all need love and attention. On one occasion, she accepted an adolescent, Caucasian girl into her home who had problems with lying and stealing. My friend did not mind this because she had dealt with girls with similar behavior issues before. The problem proved to be with the girl's caseworker. It turned out the caseworker was not comfortable placing this girl in an African-American home. This became clearly apparent from comments she would make during her visits to the home, but my friend tried to overlook them. I suggested to my friend that maybe it would be better to tell the caseworker to move the girl to another home if race was such an issue to her. My friend declined the advice and believed that everything would be okay; and it was ok for awhile until the anniversary period was over and the girl began getting in trouble and became angry.

The first indication of trouble came when the girl made a false accusation against my friend's daughter claiming she was spanked by her. Now my friend's daughter, who I have know since she was a child, was a mild mannered high school senior who I had never heard raise her voice or become angry. She was a 4.0 senior honor roll student at her high school and she had already been accepted into a major University. Nonetheless, without hesitation, the foster girl's caseworker launched an investigation and tried to have the daughter prosecuted It did not matter to the caseworker that the foster girl had an extensive record of lying and making false allegations. I couldn't help but wonder if race had something to do with it.

At the time, my friend was in the process of adopting a couple of other foster girls whom she had raised for years.. As a result of the investigation, all the foster children had to be removed from the household until the investigation was complete. The judge on the case ended up throwing the case out because of a lack of evidence. Throughout the ordeal my friend's daughter received lots of support from family, friends and school staff to help her through this terrible situation. She started college that fall and continued to excel in her studies. Her life and future plans could have been ruined by a senseless, false accusation and a bad caseworker. When the investigation was completed the foster girl was simply moved to another location with no consequences for lying. That's why false allegations are so prevalent in foster care, because there are no serious consequences for foster children who make false allegations. Many foster children use false allegations as a tool to retaliate against foster parents after being punished.

Biological parent's perspective

Foster children are not the only ones who make false allegations. Many biological parents of foster children use false allegations against foster parents to strike back at the department of social services for removing their kid(s) from them. Many of these biological parents are offended by the idea that someone else could possibly raise their children better than them so they plot to sabotage any placements in which their children are placed. I'll share an example of this. Sharon continually made false allegations against a foster home in which her daughter was placed in an attempt to regain custody. She called the police and told them that her daughter was being beaten and abused by her foster parents and said the kids were in danger. The police responded to the foster home immediately in the middle of the night and awakened everyone to investigate the abuse claim. The foster parents were shocked and embarrassed by the police presence at their house but fully cooperated. The police awakened each child, questioned them separately and checked them for bruises. After finding no evidence of neglect, the police apologized and left the residence. It turned out that the children were doing well in school and enjoyed their new home and foster parents. The biological mom was furious when her plan did not work. She was equally upset that her kids did not corroborate her story of being beaten. Nothing was done to the biological mom for making a false allegation which is why she was not afraid to continually make them. All of her children ended up remaining in foster care until the age of emancipation and not returned to her.

Chapter 10

"Catch 22"

All foster children stories are not bad. There are plenty of good, positive stories also. Beware; there is an occurrence that happens often in foster care that I call a "Catch 22." When a child enters our group home, we begin teaching the child lessons he will need to be a positive member of society. These lessons include respect, structure and discipline. Once the child learns to respect himself as well as others, his behavior improves at home, at school and in the community. When he learns structure and discipline the child becomes more organized and begins to feel capable of completing tasks with limited directions.

As I mentioned before, the majority of children who come to our group home are in special education classes at school. Often the reason for this is because their behavior is so bad, they can't effectively learn. The school separates them from the mainstream education students and keeps them separated until the child demonstrates that he can behave himself in a general education classroom and effectively complete assignments without disrupting others. Without adequate help, the child will often remain in special education classes until he graduates from high school. When the child is taught respect, structure and discipline, it becomes easier for him to stay on task and complete assignments. The child's behavior also improves and he begins to want to move into general education classes. Sometimes the child feels embarrassed for being in special education classes when most of his friends are in general education classes. Once the child begins to learn respect and self control his behavior improves and we recommend that he be moved into general education classes. Once the child is placed in general education classes more emphasis is placed on respect, structure and self control. The child generally begins to excel in class and feel proud and capable of doing work he previously thought he could not do. Here's the catch. While you are in the process of improving your foster child's behavior and teaching him how to be a good student and a positive member of society, social services may disrupt the child's progress. The child's caseworker reports the child's progress to the judge over the child's case and a recommendation is made to move the child from your home and place him in a lower level of care. This is ridiculous! Just as you begin to make progress with your foster child, the county steps in and removes the child from your home! This process has happened to us over and over again. I find it very hard to believe that moving a child from a stable environment where he is progressing to a new, unknown environment is in a child's best interest! My wife and I have had this argument over and over with caseworkers and guardian ad litems to no avail. The county believes that stepping a child down to a lower level of care and/or finding a permanent family for the child is worth the risk of destabilizing the child and possibly destroying the child's progress! Most of the children from our home who have been "stepped down" to a lower level of care have regressed back to their old behaviors and were eventually returned to a higher level of care! The main reason for the regression is because the child's progress was prematurely interrupted and the child was placed with care givers who did not know how to keep them on the right path. The county says that they are working in the best interest of the child. Moving and destabilizing a child when the child is making progress is not in the child's best interest! However, it is in the county's best interest because the lower the level of care the child is in the less the county has to pay a provider to care for the child. It still works out bad for the county and the child because the child usually ends up requiring a higher level of care than he was in when he was progressing!

Chapter 11

Bio-shock

It can be quite the spectacle to watch the county's interaction with foster children and their biological families. The process that takes place when children are place in foster care can be illustrated by the following graphic:

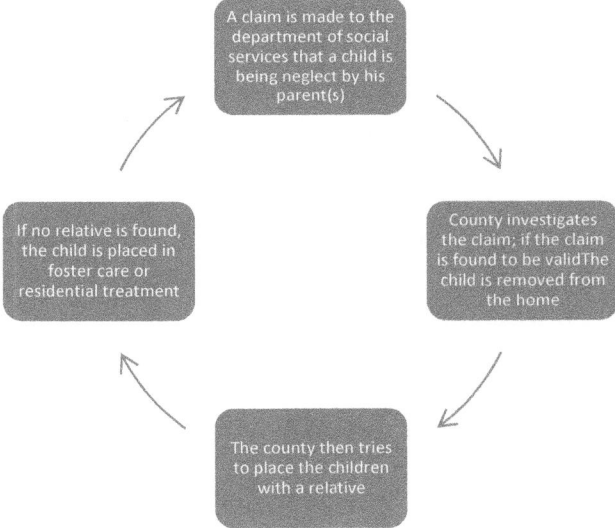

The process of children ending up in foster care can go something like this: A claim is made to the department of social services that children are being neglected by their parent(s). The abuse can be in various forms such as neglect, physical abuse, drugs, etc. The county investigates the claim. If the claim is found to be valid the county may remove the children from the home to protect the child. The county will usually try to place the children with relatives if suitable relatives can be found. This often fails. The children may be separated from one another and usually move from one foster home or residential treatment center to the next over the course of several months or years.

During this time, the county attempts to get the biological parents to complete various programs in order to get their children back. The bio-parent(s) may or may not complete the required programs. The parents who complete the programs usually get their children back. Some bio-parents get their children back and end up having them removed again because of continued neglect. When this happens, the court usually terminates the parental rights of the parents. This allows the children the opportunity to be adopted if suitable and willing adoptive parents are found. Until then, the children remain in foster care and if there are sibling groups, they are often separated into different foster homes or centers. Meanwhile, the county makes every effort to get the children visitation with each other even if the children don't ask for it or seem very interested.

Many parents whose parental rights were not terminated still have the authority to make decisions concerning what their children can and can't do while in foster care even though their children were removed from their custody. This arrangement can make it difficult to make decisions that may be best for the child. Sometimes foster children, who have been adopted or reached the age of emancipation, seek out their biological families once they are no longer under the umbrella of the department of social services. Unfortunately, many discover that their biological families are still in a severe state of dysfunction and provide no comfort or closure.

Conclusion

There are hundreds of stories like I've share concerning foster care. If you decide to provide adolescent foster care, you will have dozens of your own stories to tell, so be prepared! Providing adolescent foster care can be a heart-warming and rewarding experience for you and the child. However, you must be prepared to handle the many complications that accompany foster care. There are thousands of children in need of good, caring foster parents. If you are willing to take the risks and are good at raising children then foster care may be right for you.